invitations from the wild

Jessica Matthews

E. E.

This book begins with small things.

A winter quilt returning to the bed.
A chair warmed by afternoon light.
Keys resting in your hand before the door turns.

Each piece starts with something ordinary,
and lingers there long enough
for it to gently open.

These are not instructions.
They are quiet invitations.

To pause before continuing.
To notice what is already here.
To let a moment shift the shape of a day.

You don't need to read in order.
You don't need to finish a piece.
You can open anywhere,
and sit for a while.

Sometimes the smallest thing
is enough to let something softer in.

Summer Rain

I love summer rain.

The way it begins without much warning.

Just a soft shift in the air first,

a dampness you can feel before you can see it.

Then small drops landing on bare arms,

warm rather than cold.

Unexpected, but not unwelcome.

It starts on the way home with a carton of milk in my bag.

I could have driven to the shops.

It would have been much faster.

The milk colder.

But I chose to walk.

The bag swings lightly at my side.

The carton cool against my legs as it lightly skims.

The ground is dry enough to take the rain in immediately.

No puddles forming.

No urgency in it.

Just the quiet darkening of dust,

the smell rising slowly, as though the earth has been waiting without saying so.

There's no umbrella.

No hurry either.

I continue walking home, only softer now.

Drops gather on my shoulders,

politely resting on my shirt.

The milk feels heavier now, too.

Small water droplets gather on the side where rain has touched it.

The day had felt a little full. Pleasant, but full.

And the rain doesn't change that. It just moves through it gently.

By the time I reach home, the rain has already eased.

The ground darker than before.

The air quieter.

The milk still cold in the bag.

Not every shift asks us to change course.

Some simply move through, and we walk on inside them.

The Sunroom Window

The window in the sunroom has been left slightly open.

White paint lifting in small curls on the wooden frame.

A thin line of morning air slipping through the fly screen.

It must have been left that way overnight.

Not on purpose.

Just forgotten.

The sunroom is my favourite room in the house.

It looks straight across the garden to the uneven lawn,

the leaning fence, the beds that change each season

without much planning.

I often find myself standing there longer than I intend to.

Not doing anything in particular.

Just looking.

It may have been *me* who left the window open.

A moment of drifting that didn't quite close again.

The kookaburras found the open window before anyone else did.

Their laughter spills into the room, busy and certain, as if they're already well into the day.

Their calls softened only slightly by the mesh.

The air is cooler than expected.

Nothing rushed. Nothing announced.

Just a quiet shift that happened while no one was paying attention.

The screen does its job.

Letting some things in.

Keeping others out.

A soft kind of boundary.

Not closed. Not fully open.

Just enough.

The window is still open.

Not wide. Just enough for something to find its way in.

Sometimes what we leave slightly open

is what lets the morning find us first.

The Bathroom Tiles

Still under the blanket, the warmth is complete.

My arms folded in without thinking.

Legs heavy. Not quite ready to move, but no longer fully asleep either.

The air in the room feels fresh against the tip of my nose.

Everything else tucked in, held.

I pause.

I am not going back to sleep.

But I'm also not getting up yet.

Just resting in the warmth while the morning quietly gathers.

Eventually, I shift.

The blanket lifts slightly. One leg moves toward the edge.

The air touches skin that had been covered all night.

The warmth loosens but doesn't completely disappear.

The carpet receives my first step.

Soft, familiar, almost unnoticed.

I'm still mostly wrapped in sleep.

Still carrying the heat of the bed.

Moving slowly, without urgency, toward the bathroom.

And then I reach the tiles.

Bare feet meeting the cold all at once.

A small, bright jolt.

Not harsh, just unmistakable.

The warmth still sitting in the rest of me, while the soles of my feet register something completely different. Cool, smooth, certain.

For a moment, both are true.

Warmth held above.

Coolness rising from below.

I pause there, adjusting.

Nothing dramatic. Just the quiet awareness of contact.

Of being fully awake now,

not because of a thought,

but because of sensation.

Sometimes the coolness is the first place the new day reaches me.

The Bench

The dark wrought iron bench sits unassumingly on the front lawn.

Secondhand. A little weathered. The curves of the metal softened by time and other people's mornings.

We talked about that bench for weeks before buying it.

Not whether we needed one, but what kind.

Something worn.

Something already held by other lives.

Not shiny. Not new.

Something with history.

In the early morning, the sun finds it first.

Not the whole lawn. Just that one space.

Soft light slips through the leaves and lands across the seat, warming the metal before the day properly begins.

The bench holds the warmth differently to the grass around it.

Cool underneath. Sun-warmed on top.

A place where the body would notice the contrast

straight away.

A magpie lands nearby, tilting its head once.

A leaf drops without ceremony onto the seat.

The bench doesn't call out.

It doesn't demand to be used.

It simply waits there each morning, already in the light.

Worn.

Held.

Ready for another morning.

Some places hold warmth before we're ready for it.

Waiting patiently until we choose to sit.

The Foxgloves

The gravel path along the side of the house tilts toward

the back garden, steeper than it seems at first.

Morning sun rests on the stones,

then drifts as the house lend its shade.

The soil is rough here, pressed with dust and scattered

rock, a place where nothing should root.

And yet, three foxgloves appeared one day.

I noticed them when I was moving some pots from the

front yard to the back.

At first I assumed they were just weeds,

nothing of importance,

so I carried about my day making a mental note to

remove them at another time.

But then I paused and recognised the fragile stems, the

circular leaves, the almost velvety touch.

I knew what they were. And they were welcome here.

I lifted them slowly, a small yellow trowel from the children's gardening kit in hand.
Fingers circling roots, coaxing earth away, holding the small promise together.
They rose from the gravel, quiet, patient, delicate.

A few steps farther, nearer the fairy garden, I placed them down. Softer soil. More space for them.
Somewhere they might linger.

They settled easily. The leaves barely shifting. The stems still upright.

Three small spaces remain in the gravel.
And a few steps over, the ground holds them differently.

Not everything that grows where it shouldn't
is meant to be removed.

The Hidden Path

There's a path hidden from the road.

You wouldn't see it unless you were already looking down.

It sits off a side street I don't often walk.

A one-way road.

I usually avoid it.

I prefer tracks where I don't have to repeat my steps.

But that morning I turned anyway.

The entrance was mostly swallowed.

Low branches. Ferns leaning over.

Leaf matter pressed into the soil.

Nothing that suggests a way through.

I might have walked past it entirely.

Except the ground looked slightly different.

A small stretch lying flatter than the rest, softly worn, as if something had passed that way, not often, just enough.

I stepped through the branches.
And inside, it opened.

The path curved gently around trees,
slipped past fallen logs,
bent around moss-covered limbs.

What began as a suggestion
became a line.
What looked temporary
became shaped.

It climbed uphill toward the train line,
confidently held in the ground,
as though it had always been there
only hidden at the beginning.

You don't see where it leads from the road.

You only see enough to step in.

And then, slowly,

it becomes something you can follow.

Some paths only appear

once something softens underfoot.

The Linen Curtains

White linen curtains,
the kind I used to think were too plain.
Too neutral.
The sort you only appreciate later, when brightness feels louder than it used to.

They sit behind the heavy drapes,
the thick ones used to block out the hot sun and welcome the night.
Practical, certain, decisive.
The linen doesn't do that.
It just rests there, lighter, almost unsure of its own purpose.

They hang loosely, just off the ground, though you'd swear they touch it.
In the afternoon, the sun filters through them and softens the room.

Light moves gently across the carpet,

shifting with the leaves outside.

Sometimes it looks like quiet shadow puppets,

slow and unplanned.

On bright days, you can see out, but no one can see in.

The world remains visible, but held at a distance.

Edges blur.

Movement softens.

I usually pull the heavy drapes as the sun starts to go down, before the streetlights threaten to switch on.

Before the glass turns reflective.

Before inside and outside begin to compete.

But tonight I left them open.

The sun lowered slowly behind the hill, and the eucalyptus gathered the last of the light.

The kookaburras called first,
then the cockatoos,
then the magpies,
each one marking the shift in their own way.

The room dimmed without asking anything of me.

I closed the drapes just as the possums were waking.
The fabric falling softly into place.
The last of the light already gone.

Sometimes the light doesn't need to be blocked
to be softened.

Cut Grass

The smell arrived before the sound.
Something green drifting through the open window,
soft enough to almost miss.

The sound of the mower followed a moment later.
Low and steady, somewhere down the street.
Not close, but certainly not far.

It took a while to place it.
The wooden house at the bend.
The one with moss growing along the handrails.
Vintage pots gathered unevenly near the steps.
The garden half-kept, half-returning to itself.

The old owners left a couple of seasons ago.
The house stayed still after that.
Windows closed.
Leaves settling where they fell.

Nothing much changing.

The mower moved slowly along the slope.

Then stopped.

Then started again.

The smell drifted through once more, greener this time.

Freshly cut, but not rushed. Careful.

Something about it felt like a quiet announcement.

Not a knock.

Not a conversation.

Just a presence, gently tending the edges.

The window stayed open.

Now and then, a season arrives first as a hint

before it becomes something we can see.

The Dropped Earring

It rolled before I noticed.

A small green flicker across the floor,

then gone.

I was already running late, one earring in,

the other balanced loosely between fingers.

Not my usual ones.

Dangly, light catching along the edges.

I normally wear studs.

Something simpler.

But these had felt right this morning.

It slipped as I reached for my bag.

A soft tap, then the quiet sound of it moving somewhere unseen.

I lowered to the floor to look.

The couch sitting lower than it seems from standing.

Dust gathered in a faint line along the skirting.

A lost hair tie.

A receipt folded in on itself.

The earring rested just beyond reach.

Green against the shadow.

Still.

From here, the room looked different.

The coffee table taller.

The window cutting the light lower across the carpet.

Everything slightly rearranged by height.

I slid my hand underneath and felt the cool metal.

Light, delicate, still swinging slightly when I lifted it.

It felt strange to see it from this angle.

Something chosen in a hurry, now resting quietly

beneath everything else.

I stayed there a moment longer than necessary.

One earring in, one in hand.

The room held differently from the floor.

Then I stood, the proportions returning.

The second earring fastening more carefully this time.

Sometimes lowering ourselves to retrieve something

small changes how the whole room is seen.

The Old Library

The shop was narrow, shelves leaning slightly as though they'd settled into the years.

Books stacked upright, sideways, sometimes in small uneven towers.

Nothing arranged too carefully.

I'm not looking for anything in particular.

I just enjoy feeling my fingers trailing along the spines.

One book loosens easily.

Cloth cover, slightly worn at the corners.

No title on the spine anymore, just the faint impression where it once sat.

It opens somewhere in the middle.

The pages fall flat, as though they've done this many times before.

Inside the front cover, a stamp.

It belonged to a library,
long closed.
The ink faded but still legible,
the name of a town I recognise only faintly.

Tucked into the pocket is the old borrowing slip.
Thin card, softened at the edges.
Columns of dates, initials, careful handwriting.

A few names written fully.
Someone looping their letters slowly.
Another reduced to two neat initials.
The dates stretch across years.
The same book returning, leaving, returning again.

I turn the page gently.
The paper carries that slight unevenness older books hold.
A pause built into it.

The slip slides back into place. The book closes.

Returned to the shelf, it looks like any other.

But something about the names lingers.

All those small moments of borrowing.

Hands passing it quietly between them.

Some things continue,

even after the place they belonged to is gone.

The Kettle and the Clock

The kettle clicks on with a soft, familiar sound.
Water beginning its quiet movement inside,
not yet loud enough to claim attention.

I lean against the bench and wait.
Not reaching for a mug straight away.
Not deciding what I'll have.
Just letting the water gather itself.

The kitchen clock ticks steadily above the doorway.
Wooden, sunburst, mid-century.
Once it hung above my grandparents' mantle, facing their living room.
I used to stare at it as a child, the spokes stretching outward as if reaching for something important.

They're replicated everywhere now
but this one is original.

The ticking feels louder when I'm waiting.

Even, deliberate.

Almost racing the water as it begins to rise.

The kettle grows louder.

The clock doesn't change.

They used to boil the kettle often in that house.

Not always for a purpose.

Just because someone might want tea.

Cups appearing and reappearing across the day.

The water reaches its soft rumble.

The clock continues, unhurried.

For a moment, both move at once.

Time passing.

Water nearing.

The kettle clicks off. The clock keeps going.

I stay there a second longer before pouring.

Not every waiting needs to be filled.

Some warmth gathers on its own.

The Clothes Pegs

The breeze arrives lightly, almost unnoticed at first.

Just enough to lift one sleeve,

then another.

The washing begins to move.

Slowly.

Shirts shifting against each other.

A towel heavier than the rest,

barely lifting.

I start noticing the pegs.

Different colours, gathered over time.

Green, white, faded blue, one slightly cracked pink.

Without thinking, I match them.

A green peg for a green shirt.

White for the pale linen.

Blue for denim.

Not intentionally. Not carefully.

Just something that happens while my hands move.

I'm not bothered when they don't match.

But I like it quietly when they do.

When everything lines up without effort.

Today there are just enough pegs.

No extras clipped along the line.

No searching for one more.

The breeze lifts the clothes again.

The pegs holding firm,

colours scattered softly along the wire.

One sock turns slightly,

then settles.

The line creaks once,

then stills.

I stand there longer than needed, noticing the small order of it.

Nothing arranged. Everything held.

Movement doesn't always mean urgency.

Sometimes it's just the day passing through.

Cold Water

The glass was already there.

Left from earlier, I think.

Clear, half full, a faint ring on the bench beneath it.

I reach for it without much thought.

The glass cool in my hand, much colder than expected.

I always choose water from the fridge.

Even in winter.

Even when the tap would be easier.

It's not that it quenches thirst more.

Not really.

It just feels different.

More deliberate. More like something chosen.

The first swallow arrives quickly.

Cooler than the air, moving all at once.

Only then do I realise I was thirsty.

Not urgently.

Just quietly, somewhere beneath noticing.

The second sip follows sooner.

The water level lower than expected.

I hold the glass a moment longer.

Condensation gathering slowly near the rim.

It's a small thing, reaching for cold water every time.

Not necessary.

Not explained.

Just something that makes the moment feel slightly set apart.

Sometimes we don't notice the thirst

until something gentle answers it.

My Fellow Gardener

It lands closer than usual.

A soft weight on the fence post,

just beyond the garden bed.

A kookaburra.

Head tilted once, then again.

Watching without urgency.

I like to think it's the same one.

I can't prove it.

But it appears often enough to feel familiar.

It follows me when I garden.

Not always immediately.

Sometimes arriving after I've already begun.

I talk to it while I weed. Tell it what I'm doing.

Which plants I'm pulling, which ones I'm keeping.

I always ask it how its day is going,

it seems like the polite thing to do.

I tell it the weeding will make hunting easier later.

Clearing the ground.

Less cover for small movement.

When I move to another bed, it lifts and follows.

A short glide, then settling again nearby.

Sometimes it taps its feet lightly along the fence.

As if urging me to hurry up.

Or perhaps just adjusting its balance.

I find myself weeding longer than planned.

Not just for the garden.

For my kookaburra mate.

When I finish, it swoops down briefly.

Inspecting the cleared soil.

Then it settles again, quiet and watchful.

Not all closeness needs to be earned.

Sometimes it simply arrives and stays a moment.

The Smaller Path

The direct path is short.

A few steps across the grass, straight to the letterbox.

But the smaller path sits off to the side.

Worn lightly into the ground.

Curving past the fairy garden.

The kids made it slowly.

Back and forth,

small feet shaping something over time.

Now it feels like a real way through.

The fairy garden shifts every so often.

A new house appearing. A tiny lamp post.

Sometimes a unicorn statue leaning slightly.

The fairies arrive when the kids need them.

A small kind of magic left quietly overnight.

I always know when something new has been placed.

Still, I look.

Just in case.

Sometimes I wonder if the fairies might leave something for me too.

Not expecting it.

Just holding the possibility.

The path narrows near the edge.

A small turn around the stones.

Then back toward the letterbox.

There's nothing inside today.

Just the soft sound of the lid closing again.

I return the same way.

Through the fairy garden.

Past the tiny houses.

The long way feeling fuller somehow,

even without mail.

The longer path doesn't always lead somewhere new.

Sometimes it just lets something small be noticed.

The Glow

I don't go out at night much anymore.

Not because I don't want to.

It's just at this stage of life most of my living happens during the day.

School runs.

Coffee in the sun.

Walking the garden while the light shifts.

By evening, the house has usually folded in on itself and I stay with it.

So when I do come home after dark, I notice everything.

The street feels different.

Quieter than I remember.

The air cooler, even in summer.

The houses already holding their night.

The streetlight sits a few houses up the road, high and distant.

Its glow never quite reaches here.

Our garden stays dark, tucked slightly below the road,

as though it has slipped out of sight.

The gravel path disappears almost completely.

I walk slowly, feeling the ground more than seeing it.

The sound of each step louder than it should be.

Possums move through the trees at night.

I know they do.

Sometimes I hear them when I'm inside,

a soft rustle, a branch shifting, the quiet confidence of

something that belongs here after dark.

I wonder if I've disturbed one.

If it's paused somewhere above me, surprised by

footsteps that don't usually happen at this hour.

I find myself peering into the garden,

searching for the small reflection of eyes.

The trees hold their shapes but nothing more.

The night doesn't give much back.

Then the salt lamp appears.

A soft amber glow beyond the living room curtains.

Low and steady.

Not bright enough to light the path,

but enough to hold its place.

It sits where it always does,

warming the room from the inside.

From outside, it looks almost like a marker.

A small square of warmth in the dark.

I walk toward it without thinking.

The gravel softer now.

The garden less uncertain.

The rest of the house is still.

No movement.

No sound.

Just that gentle glow waiting behind the curtain.

I reach the steps and pause for a moment,

the light just beyond the door.

Some nights, being expected is as simple as a lamp being left on.

The Maple

The maple tree grows too close to the fence.
Close enough that its trunk presses toward the wire,
branches threading through the gaps as though the
boundary arrived later.

It's been there for decades.
Long before us.
Possibly before the fence itself.

In summer, the leaves soften the light across the lawn.
In autumn, they turn slowly, never all at once.
And in March, the cockatoos arrive.

They gather in the branches tearing at the seeds,
dropping pieces across both sides of the fence.
Their calls sharp and certain,
as though the tree belongs to them more than anyone.

The trunk sits firmly in our yard.

But half the canopy leans next door now.
Shade falling across two properties without asking.
Leaves landing where they choose.

I imagine it once stood alone.
Before the fence.
Before boundaries were measured and drawn.
Before neighbours arrived on either side.

Perhaps the fence was built around it.
The wire simply bending to accommodate what was already there.
No one wanting to cut it back.
No one quite claiming it either.

Now it stands between two spaces,
rooted in one,
reaching into another.

The cockatoos move freely through it.

The wind doesn’t slow at the boundary.
And every March, the seeds fall on both sides,
starting again wherever they land.

Some things grow before boundaries exist,
and never learn to stop at them.

The Silence

The drive to school is always full.

Shoes tapping the back of the seat.

Bags sliding onto the floor.

Someone remembering something important halfway there.

Someone else interrupting before the story finishes.

There's laughter that starts suddenly and carries on longer than expected.

Questions about the day ahead.

Observations about dogs being walked, bins left out, a cloud that looks like something I don't quite see.

I don't even think about the radio.

There isn't space for it.

The drop off happens quickly.

Doors open.

Quick goodbyes.

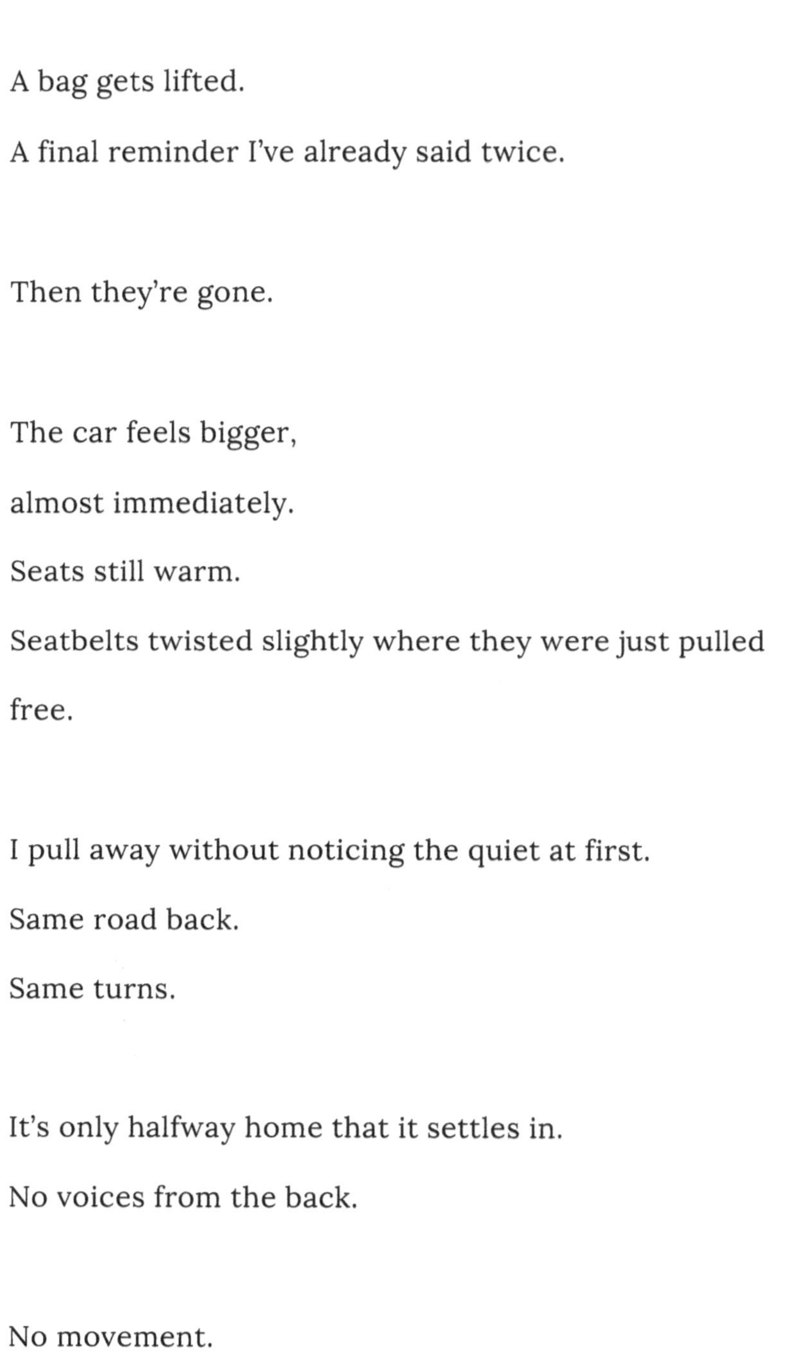

A bag gets lifted.

A final reminder I've already said twice.

Then they're gone.

The car feels bigger,

almost immediately.

Seats still warm.

Seatbelts twisted slightly where they were just pulled free.

I pull away without noticing the quiet at first.

Same road back.

Same turns.

It's only halfway home that it settles in.

No voices from the back.

No movement.

No commentary about what we're passing.

Just the low sound of tyres on the road.

The indicator clicking at the corner.

My hands steady on the wheel.

My fingers move toward the radio without thinking,

then stop.

There's nothing missing.

Just space where something was.

I pass the same houses we noticed earlier.

The same parked cars.

The same stretch of trees.

Everything looks unchanged.

Only the sound has shifted.

Sometimes the silence doesn't arrive until something

joyful leaves.

The Clouds

The clouds move quickly today.

Not drifting.

Not slowly unfolding.

Just long stretches shifting across the sky.

I don't see shapes in them.

No animals.

No hidden cities.

No faces appearing and dissolving.

I never really have.

Instead, I find myself watching the speed.

Trying to judge the wind by how fast they pass.

Noticing where they thin.

Where they gather.

I wonder if rain will follow.

Whether the garden needs a drink.

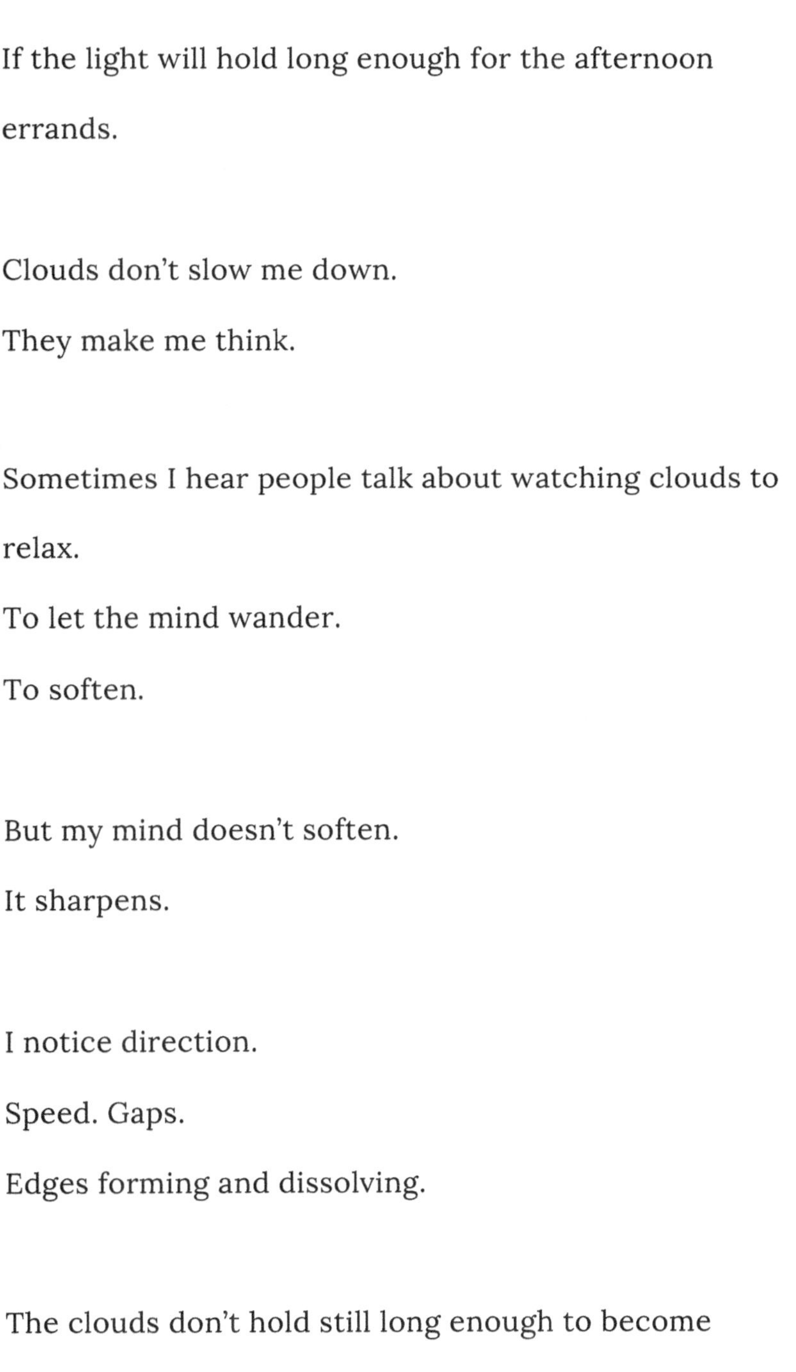

If the light will hold long enough for the afternoon errands.

Clouds don’t slow me down.
They make me think.

Sometimes I hear people talk about watching clouds to relax.
To let the mind wander.
To soften.

But my mind doesn’t soften.
It sharpens.

I notice direction.
Speed. Gaps.
Edges forming and dissolving.

The clouds don’t hold still long enough to become anything.

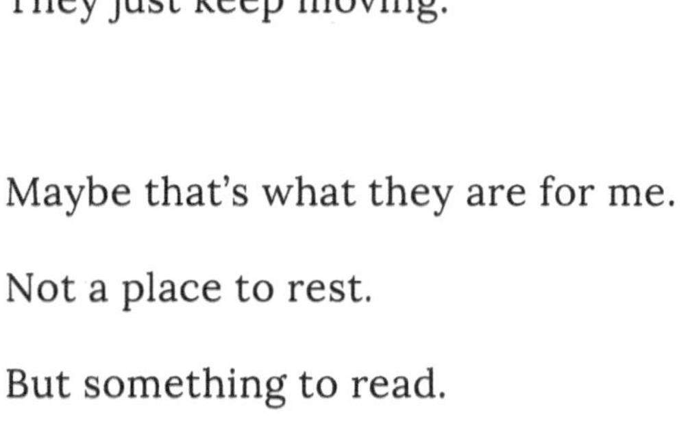

They just keep moving.

Maybe that's what they are for me.

Not a place to rest.

But something to read.

Not stillness.

Just attention.

The sky shifts again,

and I keep watching

to see what it might do next.

Not all presence feels calm.

The Keys

The keys are still in my hand.

Warm from the drive home.

The metal pressed into the soft centre of my palm.

They sit loosely between my fingers.

One longer than the others.

One slightly bent.

The small plastic tag turned backwards.

The door is right in front of me.

Close enough that I don't need to step forward.

Just a turn of the wrist.

But my hand doesn't move yet.

The keys make a small sound when I shift my grip.

Not loud.

Just enough to remind me they're there.

The air outside hasn't settled.

A car passes somewhere further down the road.

Leaves move lightly above the gutter.

My bag is still on my shoulder.

The strap pressing in slightly.

I haven't put anything down.

I'm already home.

Just not inside yet.

The keys rest heavier the longer I hold them.

Their shape beginning to mark my skin.

Ready.

Waiting.

The door stays closed.

The garden still audible behind me.

The metal quiet in my hand.

Sometimes arriving happens

before anything is opened.

Wet Hair

The water runs straight down.

From crown to tip.

Long, dark strands gathering weight as they go.

The scent of grapefruit lifts with the steam.

Clean and bright.

Something about it feels like morning, even though the day has already begun.

I watch the shampoo slide down my back.

Across my shoulders.

Down my legs.

Then circling slowly toward the drain.

The bottles sit side by side.

Similar shapes.

Similar colours.

I pause with one in my hand, unsure.

Trying to remember if I've already used it.

If I'm repeating something without noticing.

The water keeps running.

Nothing changes.

I rinse again, just in case.

The scent softening.

The strands heavier now.

When I step out, the air meets me first.

Cool against warm skin.

A small shiver before the towel.

My hair settles down my back.

Drops tracing their own paths.

One reaching my ankle before disappearing.

The hair dryer sits where it always does.

Cord loosely wound. Plug slightly twisted.

I leave it there.

The towel takes most of the water.

Not all of it.

Just enough.

Wet strands rest against my shoulders.

Darkening the fabric of my shirt.

Slowly, without hurry.

By the time I move into the next room,

the ends have already started to dry.

No sound.

No heat.

Just time passing quietly.

Some things settle

without being finished all at once.

The Next Page

The book has been sitting beside the bed for weeks.

Not hidden.

Not stacked underneath anything.

Just resting there, waiting in plain sight.

I've wanted to read it for a long time.

I remember picking it up months ago.

Maybe longer.

Thinking I'd start that night.

But evenings filled.

Shoes left by the door.

Lunchboxes rinsed.

Small conversations stretching later than expected.

By the time I returned to the bedroom,

the light felt softer.

The book stayed closed.

Tonight, I pick it up properly.

The cover warmer than I expect.

The spine firm, not yet loosened by reading.

The first pages turn easily.

Acknowledgements.

A blank page.

The start of the first chapter.

I read slowly.

Not because the words are difficult.

Just because it's been a while since I've read like this.

The room is quiet around me.

No one calling from another space.

No half-finished task waiting nearby.

The page ends midway down.

A natural pause in the paragraph.

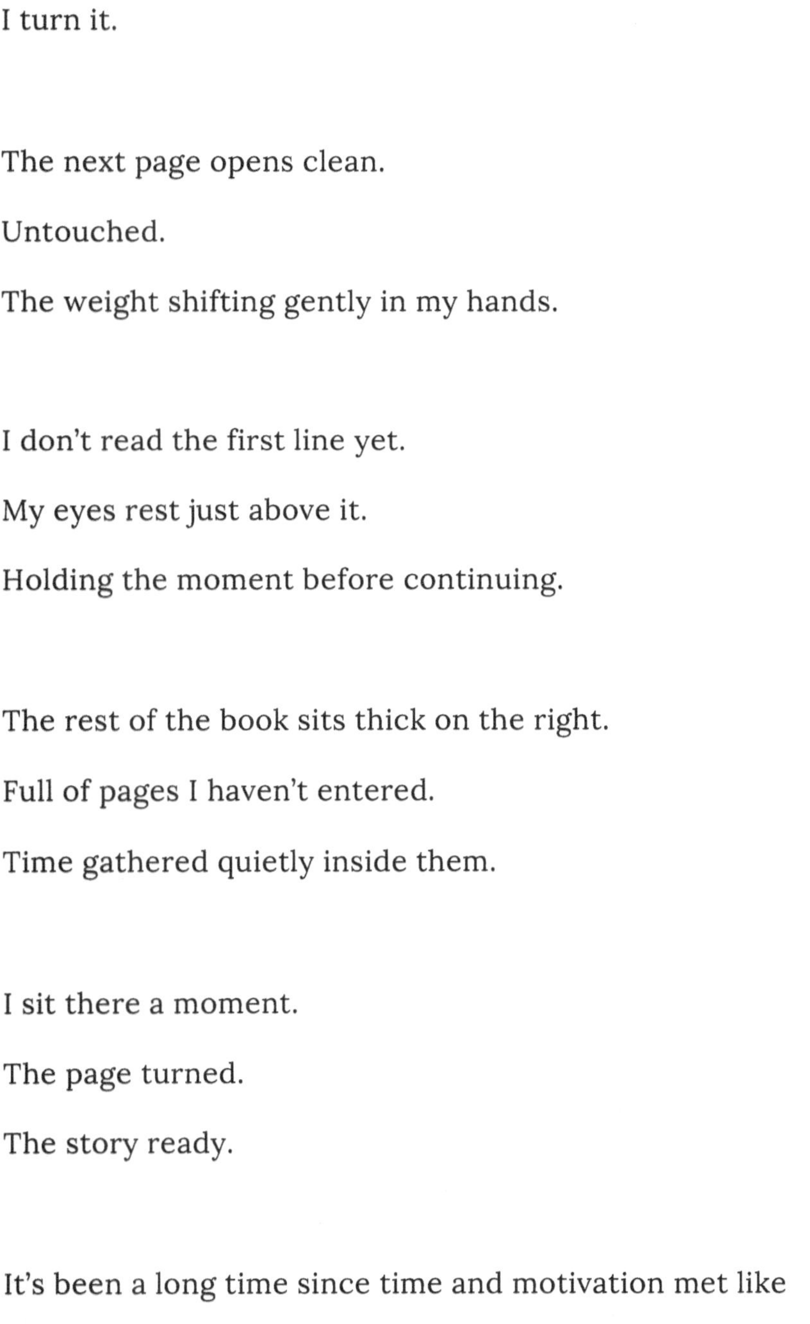

I turn it.

The next page opens clean.

Untouched.

The weight shifting gently in my hands.

I don't read the first line yet.

My eyes rest just above it.

Holding the moment before continuing.

The rest of the book sits thick on the right.

Full of pages I haven't entered.

Time gathered quietly inside them.

I sit there a moment.

The page turned.

The story ready.

It's been a long time since time and motivation met like this.

Nothing else pressing forward.

No need to hurry through.

The new page waits.

Still and certain.

The words not going anywhere.

Sometimes the turning happens

before the reading begins.

Red Roses

The mugs sit close together in the cupboard.

Stacked, mismatched, gathered over time.

Some thick. Some chipped. Some heavier than they look.

I usually reach for the sturdy ones.

The kind that feel solid in the hand.

The ones more likely to bounce than shatter if dropped.

They're practical.

Comfortable.

Easy.

Today my hand moves past them.

To the back corner.

The china mug sits slightly apart.

Off white, with small red roses circling the sides.

The gold along the rim worn thin in places.

It belonged to my grandmother.
Part of her favourite set.
The one brought out for afternoon tea.

I don't think I've ever chosen it on purpose.
It feels too delicate.
Too careful for ordinary mornings.

The handle is smaller.
My fingers closer together.
The porcelain thin beneath my thumb.

I place it on the bench gently.
More aware of the sound than usual.
The soft tap as it meets the surface.

The kettle begins to warm.
Steam rising slowly.
The mug waiting where I left it.

I fill it almost to the top.

The china holding the heat differently.

Warmer sooner.

Lighter to carry.

I move more carefully without deciding to.

One hand steady beneath it.

The roses turning slightly as I walk.

The tea looks the same.

The steam the same.

Just held in something quieter.

The mug rests in my hands.

Thin.

Delicate.

Still.

Some mornings, the choice shifts

without needing a reason.

The Purple Jacket

The jacket hangs near the end of the rail.

Between practical coats.

Muted colours.

Reliable fabrics.

This one is different.

Deep purple.

Slight sheen in the light.

A fabric that moves more than it needs to.

I've had it for years.

Picked it up without much thought.

Certain I'd wear it often.

But it always feels a little too much.

Too bright for school drop-offs.

Too soft for errands.

Too noticeable for ordinary days.

So it stays there.

Sliding slightly as other jackets are taken down.

Returned again to the same place.

This morning my hand reaches for it.

Not deliberately.

Just something different.

It's lighter than I remember.

The lining cool against my arms.

The shoulders settling into place.

The colour shifts in the mirror.

Darker indoors.

Brighter near the door.

I button it slowly.

The fabric folding neatly.

More structured than my usual coats.

Outside, the air is the same.
The street unchanged.
Bins still waiting to be brought in.

The jacket moves when I walk.
A soft swish at my sides.
The purple catching small pieces of light.

No one notices.
Nothing unusual happens.
The morning continues.

But I feel it there.
The weight slightly different.
The colour held around me.

I keep it on longer than expected.
Even once the car warms.
Even once the sun rises higher.

The sleeves settle at my wrists.

The fabric softening as I move.

Some things wait quietly

until an ordinary day wears them.

The Cicadas

The sound meets me halfway down the stairs.

Sudden, but already established.

As though it has been waiting there all afternoon.

Cicadas.

The garden looks unchanged.

Leaves still.

The air warm, but not quite summer yet.

The sound fills everything anyway.

Layered.

Constant.

Sometimes I hear them before I even feel summer begin.

Before the long evenings settle in.

Before the grass pales at the edges.

The sound arrives first.

I pause on the step, listening.

Trying to find where it's coming from.

One tree louder than the others.

But it doesn't hold in one place.

It spreads across the whole yard.

Close, then distant, then everywhere again.

I've searched for them before.

Standing quietly beneath the branches.

Eyes tracing the bark.

The sound feels near.

Then disappears.

Then returns behind me.

Sometimes I find their shells instead.

Clinging to the fence post.

Attached to the maple trunk.

Hollow. Light. Split neatly along the back.

I pick one up carefully.

The shape perfectly held.

Nothing inside.

But I've never seen one moving.

Never watched one arrive.

Only heard them.

The hum thickens as the light softens.

The garden lowering into evening.

The stairs still warm beneath my feet.

By the time the sky begins to fade,

the sound feels settled in.

As though it belongs here already.

Summer, arriving first

as something you hear.

The Shared Shade

The shade sits just beyond the path.

A wide patch beneath the tree, cooler than the rest of the afternoon.

I step into it without thinking.

My breathing is still uneven from the run.

Shoes dusty.

The warmth of the road lingering in my legs.

I take a sip of water.

The bottle slightly squeezed in my hand.

Cold against the back of my throat.

For a moment, I stand there.

Not stretching.

Not checking the time.

Just letting everything settle.

That's when the dog comes over.

A Cavalier King Charles Spaniel.

Black, red, and white in soft, uneven patches.

The colours gentle rather than bright.

It approaches without urgency.

As though the shade belongs to both of us.

As though it's done this before.

It lowers itself onto the ground nearby.

Close enough to share the cool patch.

Not close enough to touch.

Its ears fall heavily at the sides of its face.

Long, slightly wavy.

The fur darker where it gathers.

The jowls are soft.

Resting loosely as it breathes.

A calm, steady rhythm.

There's a small black dot on the top of its head.

Perfectly placed.

Still.

It looks up once.

Dark eyes, kind and certain.

Familiar in a way I can't quite place.

My old dog used to sit like this.

Quietly beside me.

Not asking for anything.

This one shifts its paw forward.

Settling deeper into the grass.

Content to stay.

The shade holds us both.

The sound of my breathing slowing.

Leaves moving lightly overhead.

Somewhere behind, a lead trails loosely.

A figure further up the path.

Unconcerned.

I take another sip of water.

The bottle cooler now.

My shoulders dropping.

After a moment, the lead tightens gently.

The dog stands without hesitation.

Turning back the way it came.

The shade feels wider again.

The ground unchanged.

Only the space beside me empty.

I finish the last sip.

The run already softening at the edges.

Some pauses are briefly shared.

The Cockatoo Feather

It's resting on the car seat when I open the door.

Just near the edge.

Where I usually place my bag.

White, soft, unmistakable.

A cockatoo feather.

I don't remember seeing it earlier.

The seat was empty when I left.

Nothing there to notice.

It must have travelled in quietly.

Caught on clothing.

Slipped inside when the door opened.

I pick it up carefully.

Longer than I expect.

The fibres clean and even, tapering to a soft point.

Cockatoos aren't my favourite birds.

They arrive in loud groups.

Tearing at the garden without hesitation.

They snap fresh shoots.

Scatter bark.

Leave half-chewed stems behind.

Sometimes they screech just as I'm getting the kids to bed.

The sound sharp against the settling house.

Unconcerned with timing.

They move through like noisy sidekicks.

Uninvited.

Certain of their place.

But the feather in my hand is quiet.

Perfectly shaped.

Soft along the edges.

The white catches the light differently up close.

Subtle greys running through the centre.

The stem pale and smooth.

It feels strange to hold something so calm

from something so loud.

I turn it once between my fingers.

The fibres shifting gently.

Weightless.

Outside, the street is ordinary.

No birds overhead.

No sign of where it came from.

I place it on the dashboard.

It moves slightly when the car starts.

Then settles.

By the time I reach the end of the street, it's still there.

Quiet and unchanged.

Some things carry beauty

without softening their noise.

The Pot

The pot is still warm when I place it in the sink.

A small coil of spaghetti clinging to the side.

Sauce gathered near the rim.

Dinner came together quickly.

Water boiling while I balanced a child on my hip.

Steam rising around us both.

It's an easy meal.

Something that fills the space when the evening narrows.

No planning. Just familiarity.

The plates rest beside the sink.

Forks laid across them.

The table wiped but not fully cleared.

I usually wash everything straight away.

Before the sauce dries.

Before the kitchen cools.

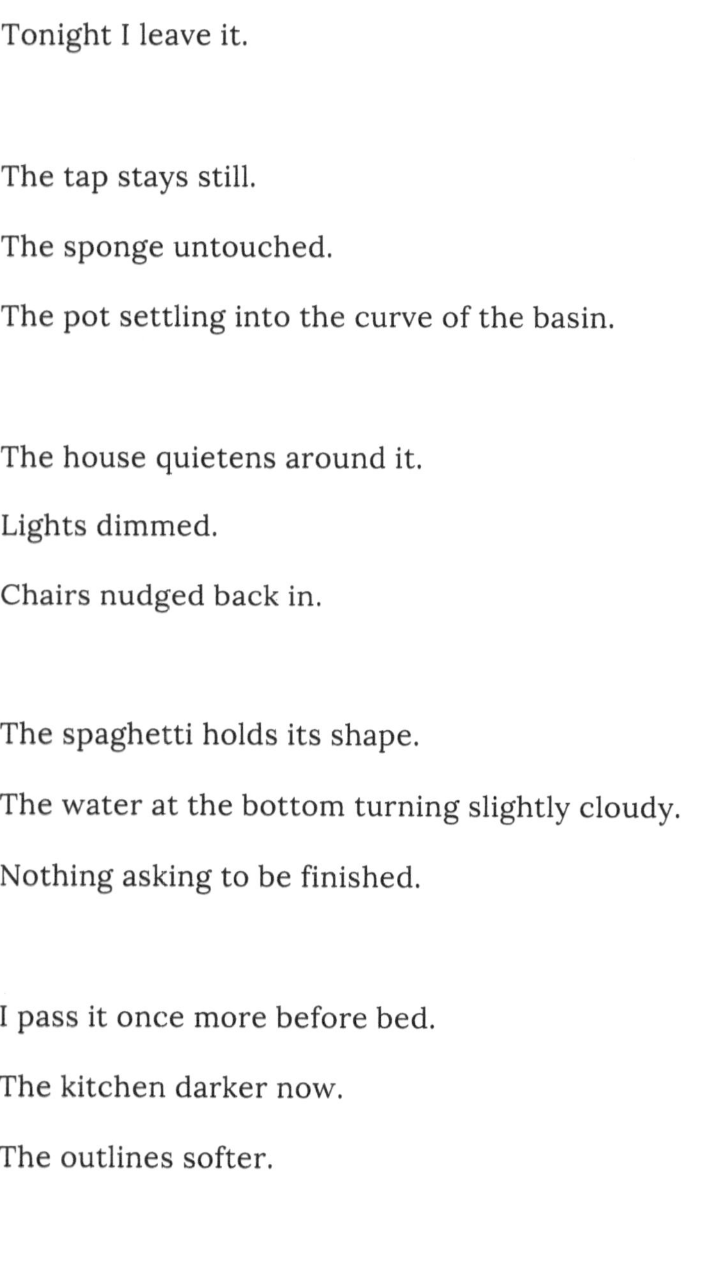

Tonight I leave it.

The tap stays still.

The sponge untouched.

The pot settling into the curve of the basin.

The house quietens around it.

Lights dimmed.

Chairs nudged back in.

The spaghetti holds its shape.

The water at the bottom turning slightly cloudy.

Nothing asking to be finished.

I pass it once more before bed.

The kitchen darker now.

The outlines softer.

In the morning, it will loosen easily.

Warm water lifting what stayed overnight.

No trace of waiting.

For now, it rests where it is.

Part of the evening still.

Some endings

are left gently for tomorrow.

The Accidental Coffee Date

The table wobbles slightly each time I shift my elbows.
One leg uneven on the pavement.
Rocking softly, then settling again.

I've taken the outside seat.
Laptop open.
A cornflake cookie resting beside my cup.

The coffee is hot enough to fog the rim.
Steam lifting in slow threads.
Cars passing further down the street.

I came for quiet.
A small pocket between things.
Just enough time to write.

Footsteps move past now and then.
A chair scraping.
Someone ordering inside.

Then laughter approaches.

Light and bright, before I see where it's coming from.

A grandmother and her grandson walk along the pavement.

He darts slightly ahead.

She reaches for him, not quite catching.

They laugh again.

The sound spilling easily between them.

Uncontained.

They pass close to the table.

The wobble shifting as they move by.

The cookie untouched.

The boy says something I don't hear.

She bends slightly as she answers.

Another burst of laughter.

Then they're already further down the street.

The sound trailing behind them.

Softening as it goes.

The quiet returns gradually.

Coffee still warm.

Screen still open.

I continue writing.

The moment folding gently back in.

Some quiet spaces

make room as they pass through.

Jasmine Tea

The teapot sits on the top shelf, white and delicate.
A neighbour gave it away in a community swap long ago.

It's the kind of teapot that waits for days that arrive
slowly, like today, when the house is mine,
and I can take the time to notice the small things.

I carefully retrieve it from the shelf as I wait for the
kettle to boil.

I choose a jasmine teabag,
soft, subtle, fragrant.
Normally I reach for something stronger, darker, heavier,
the kind of tea that demands attention and alertness.

But today, the cup, the teapot, the day itself
seem to ask for softness.

I fill the teapot carefully.

Steam curls above the spout,
wisps moving like smoke in slow motion.
I wonder why it turns like it does.
Probably something to do with the heaviness of air and
the contrast of hot and cool,
or something equally as unromantic as science.
I like to think it's a dance.
Something invisible that moves just for me.

I watch it rise,
bending in invisible currents,
and for a moment, I feel unhurried,
as if the day itself has slowed to match the rhythm of the
vapour.

The cup receives the tea, delicate warmth in my hands.
A quiet inhale, the scent pressing gently against my nose.

I take a sip, and the house stays still around me,
though the world outside carries on its usual motion..

Sometimes the day feels like this—

small, soft, a pause before the world calls again.

The Quilt

The quilt is folded at the foot of the bed.
It belonged to my grandmother, hand-stitched long ago,
each square slightly uneven,
each seam pulled tight by careful fingers.

It isn't heavy.
Not warm enough for the cooler nights.
But just enough when two warm bodies share the bed,
when warmth gathers quietly
and holds itself there.

I pull the heavier quilt from the linen cupboard,
machine-stitched, dark green,
as deep as the camellia leaves outside our window.
It smells faintly of cotton and cupboard air,
of seasons that have passed
without announcement.

The summer quilt slips aside reluctantly, soft, familiar,

memories folded into every square.
It has learned the shape of our sleep.
It knows where our feet find each other.
It knows the gentle weight of late nights
and slow mornings.

I tuck the new quilt over us,
its weight a quiet insistence,
a reminder that the season has shifted
even if we haven't quite admitted it yet.

The air tastes cooler.
The night stretches longer.
And the window frames the leaves,
still catching the last light of day
as if holding onto something
that is already leaving.

Sometimes change doesn't arrive all at once.

Sometimes it slides in gently,

settling at the edge of things.

Just enough to be noticed.

Just enough to begin.

The Outside Cushions

I don't have outside cushions.

I don't always know it's raining until it is.

By then, cushions would be wet, heavy, damaged.

A small luxury I never seem to have the time or energy for.

But my parents do.

Chairs tucked under the pergola, cushions in place.

Soft, thick, reliable.

They can go in and out with the weather,

without care, without fuss.

I sit for a moment, just to catch my breath.

The cushions are warm from the sun, even though the air has turned cooler,

slightly damp with evening dew.

The chair beneath me isn't perfect wood or shiny metal.

It doesn't matter.

Comfort arrives anyway.

I think of the work it must take,
to look after these things,
to give them a life that keeps pace with seasons.
And yet it feels effortless.
The cushions sit patiently, offering warmth without
asking anything in return.

I imagine my own garden one day,
chairs that are soft and ready,
resilient enough to stay out in sun and rain.
Not just for visitors,
not just for a fleeting hour in the afternoon,
but for the quiet, ordinary moments
where sitting down feels like a small ceremony of rest.

For now, I take a breath here,
enjoying the warmth that belongs to someone else,
letting it settle around me,
soft, steady, patient,

like the kind of comfort you carry with you

before you even realise it.

Sometimes I wonder if this is why I always feel lighter

here,

if chairs can hold comfort the same way people can,

and from time to time, I let myself sit a little longer,

just breathing it in.

Rain on the Roof

The cat curls in my lap,
soft weight against my chest as I settle into the chair.
The children are asleep,
and the house has finally become mine for a moment.

Drops begin on the roof,
soft at first, then louder,
drumming a quiet rhythm overhead.
I don't need to do anything but listen.
The cat twitches his ears, eyes half-closed,
as if he has been waiting for this sound all day.

The pen moves slowly in my hand,
thoughts following the cadence of the rain,
words spilling on the page without urgency.

Outside, the world darkens;
inside, we are warm, settled, uninterrupted.

The house exhales around us.

The dishwasher hums softly in the distance.

A floorboard creaks as the night settles deeper.

The rain keeps time, steady and forgiving,

as if reminding me that nothing needs to be hurried.

I don't reach for my phone.

I don't check the clock.

The page fills slowly, the cat growing heavier,

the rain softening the edges of everything that felt sharp today.

Sometimes the night feels like this,

a soft hush descending while everything else pauses.

And for a while,

I let myself disappear into it.

The Kitchen

The smell reaches me before I even step into the kitchen.
Rich, fragrant, familiar.
Something from my grandmother's cookbook,
a dish I never noticed as a child
but now carries memory and meaning in equal measure.

Mum moves about, small motions I watch quietly:
stirring, tasting, humming softly,
the clatter of utensils almost lost in the scent itself.
The house feels alive,
but in a different way than when I was young.
Older.
Appreciative.
Patient.

I breathe it in, letting the aroma fill the room,
fingers unconsciously tracing the edge of the table.
This smell doesn't demand; it invites.
And I let myself linger in its warmth.

Steam curls gently from the pot,

clouding the window just enough to blur the outside world.

The radio murmurs in the background.

She doesn't notice me watching,

and I don't interrupt the rhythm she has settled into.

I don't remember being this present when I was younger,

when this scene was taken for granted.

Then, it was just dinner.

Now, it feels like inheritance.

The recipe isn't written down in front of her.

It lives in memory,

in handfuls and instinct,

in pauses that only she understands.

Sometimes home arrives in smell alone,

a reminder that we carry it with us,

even when the years pass.

And sometimes,

it's enough just to stand quietly in the doorway

and breathe it in.

Lawn Daisies

The grass is freshly cut,
short, crisp underfoot,
but the daisies remain, stubborn, cheerful, scattered
across the lawn.
I sink my toes into the earth, cool and damp.

Some might see weeds, neglect,
but I see small moments of sweetness.
I bend, almost thinking of making necklaces,
but let the flowers lie instead,
tiny suns at my feet, careless and free.

I stay a little longer than I intend,
letting the garden press its rhythm into my soles,
the smell of grass and soil rising with each breath.
A child's laughter echoes faintly in the distance,
the world quietly continuing around me.

A bee drifts lazily between the flowers.

The breeze shifts the clippings into soft green lines.

Somewhere, a gate clicks shut.

Nothing remarkable, and yet everything feels held.

The earth feels steady beneath me.

Uncomplicated.

Grounded in a way I forget when I move too quickly.

I don't pick the daisies.

I don't tidy the edges.

I let them remain scattered and imperfect,

a small rebellion against neatness.

Sometimes the smallest things beneath our feet

hold the most joy.

And sometimes,

standing still is enough to find it.

The Bonsai

The bonsai moves with me.

A gift from my father, it lives in a pot,

following the sun as the seasons shift.

Most of our garden is rooted, fixed, permanent.

Not this one.

It wanders slowly, a grey nomad on a tiny adventure.

I lift it carefully,

tilting the pot just enough to catch the sunlight,

watching leaves stretch toward warmth.

It settles back down, the soil shifting slightly,

a quiet promise that it will grow wherever it lands.

Each new position feels temporary,

a pause rather than a destination.

Morning sun on the deck.

Afternoon warmth near the fence.

Sometimes inside, when the wind turns sharp.

I think of my father,
of his own wanderings across the country,
and I smile at the small, portable freedom of this tree.
Its movement isn't dramatic; it's deliberate, patient,
an unspoken conversation between earth, sun, and sky.

The trunk twists gently,
shaped by time rather than urgency.
Nothing about it is rushed.
Nothing about it is fixed.

I brush a fallen leaf from the soil,
turn the pot slightly,
and leave it to find its light again.

Sometimes we need to move just slightly
to let life catch the light.
And sometimes,
home is simply wherever we choose to place
ourselves next.

Thank you for spending time with
these quiet moments.

If you'd like to find more like this,
you can visit:

www.wildwomanpress.com.au

Jessica Matthews
Wild Woman Press

www.ingramcontent.com/pod-product-compliance
Lightning Source LLC
Chambersburg PA
CBHW021332060726
47591CB00006B/1987

* 9 7 8 1 7 6 4 5 8 4 6 1 6 *